Offered by:

Ask the HR Lady
1028 South Bishop, PMB 223
Rolla, MO 65401
877-608-4563
www.AskTheHRLady.com

ISBN 1449588220
EAN-13 9781449588229

50% of the author's royalties are donated to:
The Oprah Winfrey Leadership Academy

For
my husband and children.
I love you with all my heart.

Table of Contents

Introduction

Let's talk about what no other Human Resources person or hiring manager would ever take the risk to tell you.

In today's workplace, employers have a valid, healthy concern not to say too much for fear of saying the wrong thing and getting sued. Unfortunately, the information they "can't say" is vital to your success in getting the interview and getting the job.

Maybe you are just starting your job search. Maybe you've been at it for a long time and have not yet received an interview or job offer. Wherever you are, this book is for you.

All the best guessing in the world cannot teach you what you are about to learn. I wish you much success and hope this book is helpful to you.

MLBROXTON

Special Thanks

Randall Arthur

Tom Awtry

Dr. Anne DeLaunay

Theresa Dodson

Dr. Eph Ehly

Floyd & Joyce Huffman

Bob Mangeot

Melinda Manzo

Valerie Maxwell

Jeff Sandquist

Elizabeth Skyles-Jordan

Pamela Oakes-Skyles

Gary & Bonnie Wallbaum

Also, a note of thanks to Kent Thiry, Joe Mello, Lisa Joins, and the other fine folks who chart the course of **DaVita, Inc**. I learned more about how to be a great person and leader while in your organization than any other time in my life.

Chapter 1: A Handy List

You may be just starting your job search. Or, you may have been searching for a long time. Wherever you are in the process, the list below can help you increase your success getting a call...... getting an interview and, ultimately, getting the job you want.

Here are some items that can be accessed for free at your local library:

- ✓ Computer
- ✓ Access to the internet
- ✓ Printer
- ✓ Fax machine
- ✓ Newspapers and magazines with job ideas
- ✓ Books to help you improve your skills and understand the marketplace

Other items you will need:
- ✓ An electronic copy of your resume in Microsoft Word and Adobe format
- ✓ Simple, blank inside thank you cards. Stick with card sold in packs of 8 or so with the words "Thank You" on front. It's best to stay away from kitties, flowers, etc. Keep it professional.
- ✓ Good black pen. I suggest Bic fine point gel pens. This is for handwritten thank you cards and applications in hard copy. Carry it with you to the interview and any time you will be filling out an application. If the pen they provide to you is poor, using a great pen will make your application stand out against all the others.

✓ A phone number where you can be reached. The voicemail must say your name and deliver a short, informative greeting. Long songs or greetings can cause the potential interviewer to get frustrated and hang up without leaving a message. This phone should be on and activated as a top priority.

✓ An email address indicating your name that you can check daily. Stay away from strange or risqué email addresses. Johnsmith123 @hotmail.com is an example of a good email address while job hunting.

On The Phone: Tips for making a great first impression:

✓ Get in the habit of answering your phone in a positive way. It can ruin your chance of an interview by answering the phone with no energy, or giving a sloppy, negative greeting.

✓ A simple upbeat hello is great.

✓ Stay away from "yello!?, who dis?" or a greeting for who you *think* is calling you (i.e. Girl, you won't BELIEVE what so and so just did!)Recruiters least favorite is probably the person who sounds like they have the energy of a slug... all breathy and slow. It immediately makes the recruiter think ahead to you talking like that to customers and having low productivity on the job.

✓ When someone asks to speak to you by name (i.e. "May I please speak with Sally?") The correct grammatical response is "This is she"

Chapter 2: Where to Find Job Opportunities

I am always surprised when someone tells me they are looking for a job and have not utilized the internet, local newspapers, and their network of contacts. These are great resources that are fairly easy to access and could lead to that next great job!

Internet: You can go to Google.com and type in "find a job". Many links will come up and you are welcome to try any or all of them. I recommend the following as the two that are most used by U.S. Employers:

www.Monster.com

www.Careerbuilder.com

To effectively use these sites, you will need a copy of your resume and cover letter in Microsoft Word format.   Both sites will ask you to complete some basic information to create a profile.   I highly recommend uploading your resume and cover letter. This allows you to apply online immediately for jobs with just a few simple clicks of your mouse. Some employers only allow job seekers to apply online and do not provide phone, fax or email, so it will be important to have your profile available when you need it.

Newspaper: Your local newspaper likely has a classified section that has a "help wanted" section. This is a terrific resource for your job search. If you use this method, it will be important to keep notes about which jobs you have applied for, etc. so that you are not applying for the same job multiple times or accidentally not applying for a job.

Network of Contacts: Sometimes folks are hesitant to use this resource and I can understand why. The key is to be strategic and tactful in *how* you go about it.

What is a network? It's basically everyone you know. This includes people who are friends of your friends. A few examples of who would be in a typical network:
> Family members
> Friends
> Church acquaintances
> Former co-workers and bosses
> Social Media: Facebook, Twitter, My Space, etc.

What do you say to the people in your network? Keep it simple, keep it honest, and keep it light.

If in person, you might say "Hey, I just wanted to let you know I'm looking for a job in _____. If you hear of anything, let me know, ok?"

If via email, you might say "Just a quick note to let you know I'm looking for a job in _____. My resume is attached – would you please let me know if you hear of anything? You're also welcome to forward my resume to anyone who might know of a great opportunity."

Want to stay with your current employer? Chances are, they have a place where they post open jobs. Ask your Human Resources department where those job postings are and what the requirements are to apply for a job within the Company.

Some companies have policies about letting your current boss know when you have posted for a job. Unless the policy is very strict and would keep you from getting the job if you *didn't* tell your boss, I recommend weighing your options on this one. Only the top bosses could learn that you're looking for another job and still treat you the same. Sometimes a boss can get really ticked off and it could actually cost you your job. Tread carefully if you consider telling your boss you're looking for another job.

My recommendation is to tell your boss once you have a signed offer and give two weeks notice that you are transferring to a different department. You will still be around if they have questions after that two week period, plus, if you were quitting the company a standard notice is still two weeks.

Eric's Story

A few years ago, my friend and I were team interviewing a candidate for a supervisory position. Mid-way through the interview questions, we began to have a hunch that this guy had a story regarding his former employment. A juicy story.

After asking a follow up question or two, he told us he had been "let go".

I asked my favorite question of all time "What Happened?"

As it turns out, he was a former pastor who had been fired by his church for improper use of the internet at work. Yes, pornography.

Chapter 3: Your Excellent Resume and Cover Letter

There are some excellent resources online with regard to your resume. I personally can recommend the resources on www.Monster.com and www.Careerbuilder.com. They can take you through some great technical aspects of what to have on your resume and how to structure it.

Here are some tips from someone who looks at resumes for a living:

1. Keep your resume two pages or less. You want to be more detailed about your most recent work and less detailed about the work experience that's older.
2. Keep in mind – the employer will compare your resume and your employment application.
3. Do not put anything on your resume or application that is not true. Period. More on this in Chapter 9: The Pre-Employment Process.
4. Put "Excellent References Available Upon Request" at the bottom of the last page on your resume. Make sure to have three professional references available on a separate sheet of paper when you attend an interview. Be sure to first ask these folks if you can use them as references and it also helps to send them your resume to remind them of what you did while you worked with them. I recommend providing the following info on your employer reference sheet for each of your references:

> Reference Name
> Street Address
> City, State, Zip
> Phone #
> Email Address

5. Remember to keep your resume about your skills and experience. All information on your resume should be related to the job you're trying to get. It's inappropriate to include info that would indicate your religious preference, ethnicity, age, sexual orientation, etc. Employers are required by law to not to make decisions based on these areas of one's personal life. It makes it tough on the recruiter when you include this info because they aren't supposed to know it. Decisions are supposed to be made on your skills, experience, education and job fit.

6. If you are currently employed and don't want to chance anyone calling your current boss, create a section exactly like you would if the name was included on your resume. Then, simply delete the company name and, in the same format, type **Company Confidential**. Recruiters are used to this format and it should not be an issue.

BRIGHT IDEA: Have a friend or family member proofread your resume. You shouldn't have to explain it to them as they read it. The resume must speak for itself to an employer – they will not call you to walk them through the details.

Now, about that cover letter. Recruiters don't read it. HR folks don't read it. We want to see your resume to assess your skills and talk with you on the phone to see if your personality is a fit. I recommend using the "objective" section at the top of your resume to write a statement that shows your personal touch.

You are welcome to write the cover letter, and if you decide to write one keep it short, positive and to the point. Just understand that there is a very good chance that it won't be read, so please don't spend time agonizing over it.

"Your accomplishments speak for themselves. Unfortunately for you I'm completely fluent in exaggeration."

Chapter 4: Phone and Email Etiquette

Phone and email are the primary forms of communication for job seekers these days. Navigating through this process can be a maze that folks should take seriously. Job seekers can easily cost themselves an opportunity simply by not understanding the right way to handle this process.

Below are a few tips to help you be successful:

- Apply in the format the employer has requested. If they have an online process, do not fax or mail in your resume. It will likely not be accepted. Additionally, please do not "drop by" attempting to see someone and "put a face with a name". When folks do this, it can be really frustrating to the HR person, who is likely knee deep in solving a problem at that moment. "Dropping by" feels like the job applicant does not respect the HR person's time and can come across as a little presumptuous.
- Make it easy to reach you by phone. This is the first way most recruiters will try to reach you.
  - The number on your resume should be the fastest way to get in touch with you.
  - Make sure you have voicemail that clearly states your name.
  - Please keep your greeting message short and clear. No music, riddles,

rhymes, or listing out every member in the family "You've reached the Brady Bunch.. Kathy.. Jim.. Sharla...Susan.. etc"

- o Check this voicemail several times during the day. If you are working, check at breaks and lunch.
- o Return the voicemail as soon as possible for you to leave a professional message. You should be in a quiet place with no interruptions. As a parent, I know that it's better to wait until the kids are occupied or napping in another room before I try to return calls. Also, noisy job sites can be a distraction when the employer is trying to hear you.
- o If your "best number to reach you" is a home phone, **please make sure that members of your family understand you are waiting for an important call.** When an employer calls and has to leave a message with a person, it's always a little bit of a gamble as to whether or not the applicant will actually get the information. Many times, an employer will not call twice. **If you don't call back, they assume you are not interested.**

- o Calls from an employer need to be returned within 24 hours of *the time the employer called you.*
- What a recruiter will typically say the first time they call: "Hi, Steve, this is Susan from Company ABC. I'm calling you about the Project Manager position you applied for and would like to spend a few minutes talking with you about it. Is now a good time?" If you can talk then, fantastic! If you cannot talk without interruptions, just say "I would love to talk with you about this opportunity. Could we set up a time to talk later today?".
- Keep a log of all jobs you have applied for. The method you use is up to you, but here is what you need to know about every job:
  - o Company Name
  - o Job Title
  - o Job Advertisement (I suggest just printing this page out if online or cutting it out of the paper).
  - o All contact info from the advertisement or job posting. Why? Because people get fired, quit, and change jobs. Record ALL contact information, names and numbers just in case you need them.
  - o Keep a record of any contact you make with the employer, and any they make with you. Record the person's

- o Once you've been invited to interview, make sure to get the caller's name and number in case you have questions later.
- o Write down where you left the conversation. Are you supposed to call them tomorrow and provide info? Are they going to call you back if you get invited to another interview? This is key to keeping the process moving forward.

"We have an opening for a receptionist and a sales person and I'm ready to quit. How are you at multitasking?"

- Successful email communication. After the first phone interview, you may be doing most of your communication via email. There are a couple reasons for this, but the number one reason is it's more efficient for the employer. Here are a couple tips to help:

- o Please remove any background photos or "wallpaper" from your emails. This makes the files bigger and clogs up the employer's email. It can also make your text very difficult to read and can come across as unprofessional.

- o Use excellent grammar and punctuation. Commonly used expressions in tech talk such as "LOL, U R, OMG" etc. are totally inappropriate when speaking with an employer. You should speak in full sentences and use the same formality you would as if you were writing a letter on paper to your employer.

- o I suggest writing the email, checking any attachments to ensure they are correct, proofing everything again, and THEN adding the "To" email address. This can keep you from accidentally sending the before you are ready.

Maggie's Story

The interview was set up for 10:00am. 10:10.. no Maggie. 10:30.. no Maggie. 11:00 and still no Maggie. At 11:10 I got a call from the front desk that Maggie had arrived. I know some managers who would have turned down the interview. Believing in the goodness and imperfection of people, I interviewed her. As it turned out, Maggie M'dear was not the most qualified person for the job and was not hired. I will tell you this. If she had been up against an equally qualified candidate, her tardiness to the job interview without calling would have played a factor in whether or not she got the offer.

Moral of the Story: Plan to be early to a job interview to MAKE SURE you're on time.

Chapter 5: Giving a Great Interview

All great interviews begin well before you meet your interviewer. A great interview begins with your research of the job you're applying for and the company for which you want to work.

Thorough research, and the appropriate use of that information, is key to landing you the job you want.

Don't get caught unaware: giving a great first impression starts when you walk in the door of the building. The receptionist will have feedback about how you treated him/her.

Make sure you know the following before ANY interview:

About the Job:

What are the top 3 technical skills/job experience the job advertisement says the company is looking for in this person? Make a bullet pointed list of the experience/skills you have and use the same words the advertisement uses to describe what you offer.

What are the top 3 personality traits the job advertisement says the company is looking for in this person? Make a bullet pointed list of the personality traits you have and use the same words the advertisement uses to describe what you offer.

For Example: "Company ABC has an open position for one Billing Clerk. The successful candidate must be skilled in MS Word, Excel, and have 2+ years billing experience. Ability to work in fast paced environment a must"

Your bullet pointed list for yourself would look like this:

Technical Skills/Experience
- 4 years billing experience
- 6 years MS Word Experience. Comfortable writing letters, using mail merge, and graphics.
- 5 years MS Excel Experience. Comfortable entering data, compiling spreadsheets, writing formulas, and working with multi-tabbed worksheets.

Personality Traits
- 4 years working in fast-paced billing environment.
- Successfully met or exceeded goals/quota each month for current employer
- Ability to multi-task and prioritize many projects at one time.

BRIGHT IDEA: Make sure to have a copy of your resume for you, the interviewer, and two or three extras. You never know when you might be asked to speak with someone else so the employer can make a decision to hire you right then!

About the Company:

What does the job advertisement tell you about the Company? Most ads will give some history and info about the overall direction and purpose of the Employer. Check out the Investor Relations page of the Company website. Read the Press Releases. What just happened? What is going to happen soon? Key things to focus on are mergers, acquisitions, profitability, change in executive leadership or organizational structure, etc. Also, on the Company website check out the "About Us" section. Look for the Mission/Values. Google the Company's name. See what others are saying about this Employer.

How to use this info in the interview:

You should be able to answer these questions for yourself, if not the interviewer:

1. What significant events has the Company experienced in the past year or two?
2. What experience do you have successfully navigating through the same/similar events?
3. What significant events are coming up for the Company in the near future? How can you help the Company get there?
4. What are the Mission/Values of the Company? How have you demonstrated in your life (preferably with an employer) that your values are a match?

WOW **Factor:**

Prepare, write down, and take two or three excellent

questions with you to the interview. Most interviewers will ask if you have any questions and that is the time to show you've done your research and are excited about the opportunity. Make sure your question is specific and makes you look intelligent and curious rather than uninformed.

YIKES! Make sure your resume doesn't have a foul odor – such as cigarette smoke. This is a guarantee your resume will be thrown in the "round file" a.k.a. the trash can. I know recruiters who throw the resume away in the *bathroom* trashcan, just so the paperwork doesn't stink up their office.

At the end of the interview, if you think it's gone well, it's also ok to ask "based on what we've discussed so far, do you feel that I might be a good fit for the role of _____?" That is one way to cut down on the suspense of waiting to hear after an interview. It's not a guarantee of further consideration, but makes the interviewer stop and think. If you've had a great discussion, they are more likely to come away with strong positive feelings if they have had the opportunity to think about what a great fit you are right then. Often times, interviewers talk with so many people they might forget how good an interview really was if they wait to think about it until days later.

End on a high note

At the end of an interview, nerves may start to set in and you may have a thousand thoughts running through your mind. Stay focused and stay positive. Look the person who interviewed you in the eye and give them a big, genuine smile. Shake their hand warmly and firmly. Let the interviewer know if she/he has any questions, you'll be happy to answer them. Make sure you provide a copy of your resume on great resume paper to the interviewer. They will appreciate having your information handy to staple to your interview notes and keep for reference.

Chapter 6: What to Wear to the In-Person Interview(s)

This is something that most job seekers spend some serious cell minutes worrying about. What you wear to an interview is absolutely important and a large part of what makes up the "first impression" an employer will have of you. Being slightly over dressed will not cost you a job offer. Being under dressed, however; definitely can.

Fortunately, there are some pretty simple ways to figure out the right thing to wear. When in doubt, dress slightly better than you think you have to. Being appropriately well-dressed shows you are serious about the opportunity and have respect for both yourself and the interview process.

BRIGHT IDEA: Call the main phone number of the company and ask the front desk person what most managers wear to work. She/he sees EVERYONE and will likely be willing to help you. Keep the discussion very short, as she/he has multiple phone lines to answer and customers to assist.

Here's a simple guide to help you decide what to wear to the interview:

Hourly job paying $15 an hour or less: Khaki pants, button up shirt, and clean (preferably leather-looking) shoes.

Salaried job paying $15 an hour or less: Nice slacks, button up shirt, and clean (preferably leather-looking) shoes. Women: I suggest a shiny, conservative, low-heeled shoe.

Non-manager job over $15 an hour: Suit with jacket or very nice slacks, button up shirt, and clean, shined shoes. Women: I suggest a shiny, conservative, low-heeled shoe.

Ted's confidence quickly fades.

Manager job:

MEN: Suit with jacket, nice button up shirt, and clean, shined shoes. Tie not optional if interviewing with Fortune 500 company.

WOMEN: Same as guys or Very nice slacks, crisp button up shirt, and shiny, conservative low-heeled shoe. Keep jewelry simple and earrings no larger than a dime. *Take me seriously about the earring thing. The last thing you want is the staff to make jokes that you fell asleep in your "clubbing" earrings and forgot to change them out for the interview. It happens.*

Executive job: Exceptional suit, crisp button up shirt, shiny leather shoes. Women: I suggest a shiny, low heeled shoe.

If you are on a budget, check the "what to wear" guide above and invest in the following. NOTE: to preserve the new look, only wear these items of clothing to an interview:

MEN:
1. Well-fitting pants. Get them altered if needed. These pants should fit around your waist and you need to wear a belt. When you sit, the pant should be long enough that none of your bare leg shows above your socks.
2. Two button-up shirts that coordinate with your pants. You can wear one to the first interview and the other to the second interview. These

should be tucked in when worn to your interview.

3. Nice belt that matches your shoes.   If your shoes are black, wear a black belt.   If your shoes are brown, wear a brown belt.

4. Shoes the same color as your belt. These shoes should be shiny and unscuffed.

5. Nice dress socks. This is the same rule as the shoes/belt.   Brown shoes need brown or tan socks. Black shoes need black or gray socks.

Body Language Tips:

✓ Keep your hands at your sides or folded loosely in your lap.

✓ Avoid crossing your arms or legs. Crossed ankles are ok and can help keep your body square with your interviewer. For guys, it can help keep you from doing the spread knee sprawl.

✓ As a general rule, sit back in your chair with good, relaxed posture.

✓ Keeping your hands loosely folded in your lap, palms up, can help you stay relaxed and approachable.

✓ Look the interviewer in the eye.

✓ Lean forward, when appropriate, to show interest in the subject.

✓ Relax your face and don't be afraid to smile!

WOMEN:

1. Well-fitting pants or skirt. There should be no visible panty line. I suggest pants of a darker color (brown, tan, black, gray). Skirts should be long enough to reach the middle of your knee when you sit. Anything shorter is considered a miniskirt and is inappropriate for a job interview.

6. Two button up shirts that coordinate with your skirt/pants. You can wear one to the first interview and the other to the second interview. Preferably, the shirts should tuck in. If tucking in your shirt is not flattering, I suggest a button up suit-type jacket.

7. Nice belt that matches your shoes. If your shoes are black, wear a black belt. If your shoes are brown, wear a brown belt.

8. Shoes the same color as your belt. These shoes should be shiny and unscuffed. I suggest a conservative, shiny low-heeled shoe.

9. Nude or black panty hose. Please do not match your panty hose to your shirt or any other color in your outfit. It shows the interviewer you are out of touch with what's appropriate in key situations (such as a meeting with a big boss or high profile presentation).

Hair: A fresh haircut is fantastic. You feel great and it looks great.

If you color your hair, have a weave or braids, make sure your hair is kept up while you're interviewing. When an interviewer sees a person whose hair is a mess, it could signal that you don't manage your time well or take your commitments (or the interview) seriously.

If you have long hair, it must be off your face. You should not have to touch your hair at all during the interview.

YIKES! Clothing should be neatly ironed and stain-free. Do not snack, drink, brush your teeth or smoke in your interview clothing. Yes, I said smoke. FACT: Recruiters who do not smoke typically think that smokers have a poor work ethic and take too many smoke breaks. A smoker is less likely to be hired by a non-smoker. If you smoke, don't make it evident.

Nails:

MEN – your nails should be trimmed and clean. Fingernails should not reach beyond the end of your fingertip. I suggest 1/8" or less of white nail. Much more and the interviewer could be distracted wondering why you have long fingernails.

WOMEN – your nails should be trimmed and clean. Fingernails should not reach beyond 1/2" from the end of your fingertip. If you paint your nails, there should be no chips in the paint. If you have acrylic nails, they must be filled and neat. If you aren't able to maintain paint or acrylic, take it all off. Clean, well-kept nails are absolutely better than poorly kept acrylic or painted nails.

Make Up:

MEN: I don't suggest it unless you have a specific reason for doing so.

WOMEN: Keep it simple. I heard a rule of thumb years ago that seems to work well. Play up either your eyes or your lips, but not both. If you're doing big things with your eye shadow, etc., stay more neutral on the lips. If you're doing a really bright lipstick, stay more neutral with your eye makeup. This is not the time to make a statement with your makeup unless you are going for a really edgy, artsy job.

"You don't like your job do you?"

Chapter 7: How to Follow Up After Your Job Interview

Job seekers agonize over this one. You are going to be amazed at how simple it really is, and can be summed up in two words: sincere appreciation.

Here's what I recommend:

- The day of the interview:
    - ✓ Send an email thanking your interviewer for their time and consideration. A sample email that would be effective is: "Susan: Thank you again for your time and consideration today. I really enjoyed meeting you and learning more about Company ABC and the Project Manager opportunity. Please let me know if I can provide any further information and I will be more than happy to help. Sincerely, John Smith (555)123-4567"
    - ✓ Send a thank you card to the interviewer that says the same thing your email did.

I don't recommend any further communication unless it's initiated by the employer. Trust me, they will contact you if they are interested. Job seekers can actually lose opportunities to continue through the process by being pushy and overly aggressive with the recruiter.

Here's an exception. Let's say you had a fabulous first interview and you feel pretty sure they are going to call you in for a second interview. And let's say you get a job offer from another company, but would rather work for Company ABC. Here's what you do... you call whoever your HR/recruiter contact is and be really honest. Here's the message: "Hi, Susan, it's John. I recognize that you're probably still working through the interview process. I got a job offer today from another company but am really excited about Company ABC. Could you let me know if I'm still in the running for the Project Manager job?" If yes, ask when they anticipate making a decision. If it's going to be a couple of days, you could possibly stall the other company, but you take a risk that the other company will retract the offer. At that point, you have to make a decision about what's right for you, based on the amount of risk you can take with respect to potentially losing a job offer.

James' Story

The interview went well. The resume was good. But at the end of the day, James was not as qualified as the candidate chosen for the job. When he got the "thanks but no thanks" letter from our company, he called me and was very persistent. After leaving several messages within an hour or two insisting on a meeting to discuss why he wasn't chosen, I spoke with him and explained that he was not the most qualified candidate for the job. He repeatedly pointed out his strengths from his resume. While frustrating, it broke my heart. I will never forget it.

Moral of the Story: Sometimes there isn't a definitive reason why you don't get the offer. Brush yourself off and spend your energy moving forward toward the next opportunity.

Chapter 8: Negotiating a Terrific Offer

Recent studies have noted that there is still about a 30% gap between what women and men make for doing the same job. I believe the #1 reason this happens is in the offer negotiation process.

Here's how a job offer typically goes with a **WOMAN**:

> Employer: Congratulations! We would like to offer you the analyst position at $50K per year. Your start date will be in two weeks.

> Woman candidate: Great! Thank you! I really appreciate you letting me know and I look forward to seeing you in two weeks!

> Click.

Here's   how a job offer typically goes with a **MAN**:

> Employer: Congratulations! We would like to offer you the analyst position at $50K per year. Your start date will be in two weeks.

> Male Candidate: Great! Hey, I really need to make more in the range of $60 - 65K – is there anything you guys can do for me?

> Employer: Well, budget is pretty tight, but we could probably go up to about $57K – would that work?

> Male Candidate: It could – what is the bonus potential?

Employer: Well, we really hadn't set anything in stone... We could do an annual 5K bonus based on performance.

Male Candidate: Ok great. One other thing I was hoping you could help me with. I noticed in your benefits package that you sent over you offer tuition reimbursement.   I just finished my degree so wouldn't be needing that, but I was wondering if I could translate that benefit as a sign on to help me with the tuition I've already incurred.

Employer: That seems reasonable. I don't think we could do more than 10K, though. Would that work?

Male Candidate: Sure! Hey, just one other thing. There are some projects I need to finish up with my current employer.   Would a start date four weeks out work?

Employer: Sure. Sounds good. We'll get a revised offer out to you within the next couple of days. Let us know if you have questions, ok? We'll be happy to help. Again, welcome on board.

Click.

What just happened?   The woman negotiated nothing and got a standard offer, so she ended up starting on the employer's timeframe and getting $50K. Period. The man ended up with a total annual comp potential of $62, a sign on bonus of $10K and an extra two weeks with which to take a vacation between jobs for some much needed transition time and rest.

The old saying is right – ask and ye shall receive. Women tend to be afraid they will make someone mad if they negotiate. Men know THEY will be mad if they DON'T negotiate. Sure, it can get a little tense during the negotiation, but once it's done the benefits are long lasting. Many companies give increases based on a %. If you're already making more, your increases are larger and you make much more over time than someone starting out at a lesser base pay.

The following are some tips for the negotiation process:

1. **Know what you're bottom line is**. Just like when you're making a purchase, know what your thresholds are and don't cross them. If vacation is a deal breaker, stick to your guns and don't settle for less. You'll end up burned out and resentful. If it's money, don't get into a situation where you're miserable because you feel overworked and underpaid from the get go.

2. **Be Nice.** Negotiations should be professional, but don't let the heat of the battle get the best of you. Be nice. Even if you're making a counter to the employer's offer, find a way to be kind and friendly. Stay approachable and open to what the employer has to say. If you come to a stalemate, don't feel like you have to solve everything right that instant. Take a breath and say "You've given me a lot to think about. I'm really excited about the opportunity. Would it

work for us to touch base on this tomorrow? What's the best time for me to call you?". Get off the phone, and take a break from the negotiation. This will give both of you time to think.

3. **The old egg in the basket saying is true.** Don't put all your eggs in one basket.... if the bottom falls out, that's a scene most folks try to avoid. Even when you're in negotiations or have had a great interview you just KNOW will end up in a finalized offer, continue shopping for a job. Keep your confidence up. The very worst possible position to negotiate from is one of desperation and zero options. Know that if this opportunity doesn't work out, there will be one that does. Don't ever accept a deal breaker and ruin your sense of self and quality of life.

Darren's Story

Great internal candidate. A manager well-liked by most. Got an interview for a promotional position managing people. Resume looked great. The problem? His team didn't trust him and didn't perform well. The hiring manager turned him down for the promotional position but later moved him into an "Individual contributor" role. He was very successful and went on to do great things with his team and throughout the company.

Moral of the Story: If you're interested in doing something different, don't be afraid to interview strategically. It may turn into something good down the road.

Chapter 9: The Pre-Employment Process

This is likely the least thought about portion of the entire "get the job" process, but it can be the most likely to get you fired before your first day of work.

What is the pre-employment process? For most companies, it's the interaction and paperwork that includes completing the employment application packet and getting your drug screen/background check.

Here are some tips to help you successfully navigate through this phase of getting the job:

1. **Complete all paperwork accurately and completely.** This is not the time to skim over the paperwork and sign it. Take time to read every single document you are asked to sign or provided. You will be held accountable for knowing this information and acting according to it's instructions.

2. **Tell the truth.** In all situations. Listen, if the employer asks you something, it's not because they can't find out through the background check company. They can. This is an integrity test. They typically just want to see if what you tell them is exactly what comes up on the background check.

3. **Pay attention.** What are deadlines you need to meet? Is the paperwork due back in 48 hours? What is the timeframe you have to go take the drug test? These are steps that can inadvertently cause folks to get fired before their first day.

What you don't know CAN hurt you. Here are some slipups that could get you fired before you even start your new job:

1. **Failing your background check.** Most people don't fail because of something on their background check. Most folks fail because they lie on their application about what will turn up on their background check. Got a DUI? Just say so. Got a misdemeanor conviction? Just say so. Failure to give the information required is called "omission" and "falsification of a legal document" and will likely cause the employer to withdraw your offer of employment immediately. Another biggie is saying you have a degree when you don't. This happens a LOT. Just put "attended, did not graduate" or "anticipated graduation date: 5/1/2012" etc.

2. **Failing your drug screen.** Like to enjoy a good batch of pot brownies on the weekend? If you're looking for a job, don't do it. Most illegal drugs stay in your system for a lot longer than a few days. Sometimes folks try to delay their drug test to let the drugs "wear off" so they just won't show up and hope it gets rescheduled. Most employers will only allow about 72 hours for a

candidate to take a drug test once the candidate is notified they have to go, so failure to show up within that window of time is an automatic disqualification.

3. **Literally getting fired.** If you are already a temp for the company you're going to work for and you get fired as a temp, be prepared to have your offer withdrawn. Not all companies do this, but just be extra careful during that transition time. Some folks start thinking "what do I need this stupid temp agency for any more" and quit showing up to work or perform poorly. The problem? You're exhibiting these behaviors in the future employer's workplace and they can see it. It's happened... and it ain't pretty.

4. **Criminal conviction** If you get sent to jail and can't start your new job, get prepared to be fired before you even start work. That is just entirely too much drama for most employers to deal with right off the bat.

My Story

Right out of college. A city girl. In Iowa. I couldn't even find a job shoveling feed (I asked – they said no). So broke I couldn't even go through a drive thru for a soda. So, in my best interview outfit, I pulled over to see if I could use a bank's water fountain to get a drink. I saw a nice man in a suit and asked if he knew where the water fountain was, and if it would be ok if I used it. He said yes, and walked me to it. I explained I was out looking for a job and really appreciated his help. He asked me to come into his office for a few minutes. **He was the president of the bank and hired me that day.** I think that Tom Awtry, CEO of South Ottumwa Savings Bank, made up a job for me that day. I worked my heart out for him and never forgot the lessons he taught me. One of them is that blue and black are the most professional colors. Simple, and I have used that tidbit countless time - it works.

Chapter 10: Your First Day of Work

You made it! You've successfully navigated through getting an interview, impressing the employer, negotiating a terrific job offer, and the tricky pre-employment process. Now what?

Here are a few things to think about prior to your first day at your new job:

What to wear. It's important to dress comfortably, and appropriately. As a general rule of thumb, wear something similar to what you wore to your interview. You will be meeting a lot of new people and making dozens of first impressions. It's good to look and feel your best.

Will your car start? It's always good to make sure that whatever transportation you're going to use to get to work is reliable. If you have doubts, make a Plan B for a friend, relative or bus to get you there.

Plan to be early. If you think it will take you 15 minutes to get there, plan for 30. Some folks think "well, the employer will understand if I'm a little late... it's my first day". It's just the opposite. Employers expect new hires to be the *most* timely and full of enthusiasm

Have a plan for lunch, just in case they don't. Great bosses make sure their new employees are treated to lunch on their first day of work. Some bosses are thoughtful enough to make sure a "buddy" is assigned to each new employee to show them around for at least the first few days and eat lunch with them. Many companies/managers don't think of this, so just in case... make sure you either take your lunch or have enough money to buy something to eat.

Turn off your cell phone. You'll get a feel for what cell phone usage is or isn't ok in the days to come. Best practice is to keep your cell phone on vibrate, check it on breaks and only answer it during work time if it's a true emergency (such as you have a sick child and are waiting on a call regarding her/his health).

Request an agenda or training schedule. Managers hire because they need to fill an opening. They are likely overworked, are short-staffed, and worn out. Your first day of work is TOP priority to you, but most managers are terrible about giving new hires the attention they really need those first few days. Requesting (not demanding) an agenda or training schedule is good for you and helps set you up for success.

Request a copy of your job description. This is the *very* best time to get this document. So that your new boss doesn't mistakenly think you are a "that's not my job" type of a person, it's important how you ask this. Say, "I would like to make sure I understand what's expected of me so that I can do a great job. Could you tell me where I can find a copy of my job description?" Your boss may tell you to go to Human Resources. If so, follow up until you get what you need. The job description may change over time and you need to know what it was when YOU were hired into the job.

Make new friends! This is one of the most fun parts of any new job. You meet a whole new group of people to hang out with and have fun. Hopefully, fun is part of the culture at your new, great job. If so, there will be plenty of opportunities to laugh while working hard for that paycheck you deserve.

Epilogue

I hope you've enjoyed this quick reference job on how to get a great job. Even more so, I hope it's been helpful to you and you have had at least one "Oprah Aha!" moment. I love Oprah… but I digress.

This book was written solely with you in mind. Along with an exceptional team of nice people, who happen to be front line experts at hiring and managing employees, we focused on specific things that you will need in your job search. We asked ourselves questions such as, "What are common errors people make that cost them jobs… and they don't even know it?"

Special thanks to my loving husband and best friend, Richie, who gave excellent advice and listened to many… many readings of this book while it was being written. Also, thanks to my children, Ava and Richard, who took lovely naps and gave Mommy time to write this book. ☺

I would be remiss if I didn't also thank Elizabeth, my wonderful friend and lifelong encourager. She never seems as surprised as me whenever I accomplish good things. She has taught me to expect greatness of myself and others.

Ah, DaVita. Truly the best company I have ever worked for. Their ~~employee~~ *teammate* culture is truly world class. The most important thing I learned at DaVita is how to connect who I *want to be* with *who I am*.

About the Author

Michele Laine Broxton is a happy small business owner, author, columnist, Fox NewsRadio recurring guest, and mom. Broxton writes most frequently about business, leadership, getting organized, change management, profitability and parenting.

A philanthropist at heart, Broxton gives back to her local community in many ways including serving as an advisor to a local school board and arts society and providing free human resources support to small businesses.

Never despise meager beginnings. ~Clark Davis

Broxton was adopted infant from a children's' home in St. Louis, MO into a traditional Mid-Western family. Growing up as the child of a small business owner, Broxton developed a strong sense of what makes a business and its employees win or lose. Broxton earned a Master of Business Administration – Human Resources Management (MBA-HRM) degree and has led at Fortune 500 Companies including DaVita, Inc., Central Parking, Inc., and Owens Corning.

After recently leaving the corporate life to become a full time business owner and author, Broxton lives in the Midwest with her husband and two children.

Reading Recommendations:

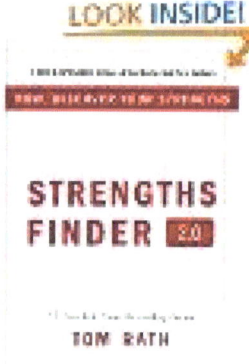

Amazon.com

Amazon.com

More.........

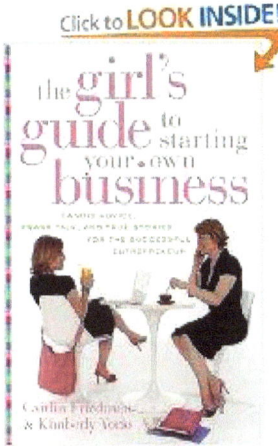

Amazon.com

Recommended Authors:

Suze Orman
Jack Welch
John Maxwell
Caitlyn Friedman & Kimberly Yorio
Jeffrey Fox

Attitude

By Charles Swindoll

The longer I live, the more I realize the impact of attitude on life.

Attitude, to me, is more important than facts. It is more important than the past, than education, than money, than circumstances, than failures, than successes, than what other people think or say or do. It is more important than appearance, giftedness or skill. It will make or break a company... a church... a home.

The remarkable thing is we have a choice every day regarding the attitude we will embrace for that day. We cannot change our past... we cannot change the fact that people will act in a certain way. We cannot change the inevitable. The only thing we can do is play on the one string we have, and that is our attitude... I am convinced that life is 10% what happens to me and 90% how I react to it.

And so it is with you... we are in charge of our attitudes.

www.ingramcontent.com/pod-product-compliance
Lightning Source LLC
Chambersburg PA
CBHW040903180526
45159CB00001B/501